Out & About in Singapore 2

Text by **Melanie Lee**

Illustrations by **William Sim**

Marshall Cavendish
Editions

© 2023 Marshall Cavendish International (Asia) Private Limited

Published by Marshall Cavendish Editions
An imprint of Marshall Cavendish International

A member of the
Times Publishing Group

Other Marshall Cavendish Offices:
Marshall Cavendish Corporation, 800 Westchester Ave, Suite N-641, Rye Brook, NY 10573, USA • Marshall Cavendish International (Thailand) Co Ltd, 253 Asoke, 16th Floor, Sukhumvit 21 Road, Klongtoey Nua, Wattana, Bangkok 10110, Thailand • Marshall Cavendish (Malaysia) Sdn Bhd, Times Subang, Lot 46, Subang Hi-Tech Industrial Park, Batu Tiga, 40000 Shah Alam, Selangor Darul Ehsan, Malaysia

Marshall Cavendish is a registered trademark of Times Publishing Limited

National Library Board, Singapore Cataloguing in Publication Data

Name(s): Lee, Melanie, 1979- | Sim, William, 1967- , illustrator.
Title: Out & about in Singapore 2 / text by Melanie Lee ; illustrations by William Sim.
Other Title(s): Out and about in Singapore 2
Description: Singapore : Marshall Cavendish Editions, [2023]
Identifier(s): ISBN 978-981-5044-30-0 (hardback)
Subject(s): LCSH: Singapore--Description and travel--Juvenile literature. | Singapore--History--Juvenile literature.
Classification: DDC 915.95704--dc23

Printed in Singapore

CONTENTS

Introduction

Dear reader,

We had so much fun with our previous book, **Out & About in Singapore**, that we decided to create another illustrated travel guide.

Welcome to **Out & About in Singapore 2**!

This book focuses on nature spots in Singapore because for us, these are some of our favourite places in this country.

While Singapore is famous for having many tall skyscrapers and shopping malls, it's also a place with much lush greenery. Did you know that around 22% of Singapore's land is covered in forest? And even though it is a small, urbanised country, Singapore has a rich biodiversity with over 2,000 plant species, 57 mammal species, 98 reptile species and 25 different amphibian species.

On a more personal note, we find that spending time with nature helps us to relax, have fun with our family and friends, and boosts our health with the physical activity and fresh air.

We hope that this book will open your eyes to all the wonderful nature teeming in Singapore!

Your fellow Singapore nature explorers,
Melanie & William

A City in Nature

Even though Singapore is a bustling city, there's plenty of greenery everywhere with pretty parks in every neighbourhood and a wide variety of nature spots. This did not just happen by chance. It started with the careful planning of the country's first prime minister, Lee Kuan Yew.

When Singapore became an independent country in the 1960s, Mr. Lee had a vision for the country to become a Garden City, with roadside greenery and tree-planting projects. At that time, he was determined that Singapore would not become a dull concrete jungle, but rather, be a city beautified by the variety and colour of plants. Even though he was very busy running a country, Mr. Lee would make it a point to personally choose specific trees and flowers to plant around the island.

Today, Singapore is one of the greenest cities in the world. The National Parks Board (NParks) helps to look after the country's natural heritage and hopes to transform Singapore into a City in Nature – a place with even more green spaces for future generations.

catoxylon Formosum
(Mempat)
anted by the
rime Minister
Lee Kuan Yew
16.6.63

Packing for Nature Outings

Going for nature outings requires planning. You can help the grown-ups with this by packing your own bag for a day out in nature!

WATER

It's important to stay hydrated as you're out and about, especially in Singapore's hot and humid weather.

CAP/HAT

There may not always be shaded areas where you're going, so bringing something to cover your head keeps you from getting too hot! Pick one in your favourite colour to wear.

SUNSCREEN AND SUNSHADES

You are going to be out in the sun for a long time, so you'd need protection from its harmful UV (ultraviolet) rays with sunscreen and sunshades.

UMBRELLA OR PONCHO

Sometimes, there can be sudden showers while you're out in nature, so it's always good to have an umbrella or poncho on standby to prevent you from getting soaked through.

SIMPLE SNACKS

Given that you're moving around so much during your nature outing, don't forget to keep your energy levels up with healthy snacks such as apples, bananas, granola bars or sandwiches.

TISSUE PAPER AND WET WIPES

It's almost expected that you'll get quite dirty and sweaty when you're out in nature. Having some tissue paper or wet wipes on standby can help you in cleaning up a little so you'll feel more comfortable.

EXTRA PLASTIC BAGS

A bag or two may come in handy when you need to clear your trash (e.g., snack wrappers), but there's no bin nearby. It's also a great way to keep wet or dirty clothes after some grubby fun in nature!

EXTRA CHANGE OF CLOTHES

You never quite know what your nature outing will be like, and sometimes, you may end up dirtier or wetter than expected. Having an extra change of clothes gives you the flexibility to try out unplanned things too e.g., deciding to splash about in the sea after hiking along a coastal trail.

EXPLORING

TreeTop Walk

The TreeTop Walk is a 250m-long freestanding suspension bridge where you can get a bird's eye view of the lush forest canopy and the sparkling waters of Upper Peirce Reservoir. It's also a great way to spot animal life in the Central Catchment Nature Reserve. You can start off your walk either from MacRitchie Reservoir (4.5km) or Windsor Nature Park (2.5km).

The Central Catchment Nature Reserve is the largest nature reserve in Singapore. It occupies over 2,000 hectares of forest and serves as a "green lung" in the centre of this island.

What can you find here?

BRACKET FUNGI

These tough and woody fungi that grow like shelves are usually found on the trunks of dead trees. Some can also end up as parasites on living trees.

LIANAS

These long-stemmed woody vines are rooted in the ground and use other trees as a form of support to climb up and get more sunlight. They are usually found in tropical rainforests.

TORCH GINGER FLOWER

Its vibrant pink flower bud doesn't just make a pretty decoration. It is also an ingredient in local dishes such as *rojak* (a kind of salad) and *laksa* (a spicy noodle dish) and helps to reduce cholesterol and constipation.

CRIMSON SUNBIRD

It won't be hard to spot this striking bird feeding on nectar or insects. Many nature lovers regard it as the unofficial National Bird of Singapore because the male bird has bright red feathers similar in colour to the country's flag.

LONG-TAILED MACAQUE

These smart and social animals usually live in groups of 30. It's best not to offer food to them, and don't carry plastic bags around openly as they're pretty good foragers!

MALAYAN COLUGO

These nocturnal creatures are usually resting on trunks in the day, but at dusk, you can catch them gliding from tree to tree, looking for leaves and flower buds to eat.

SUNDA PANGOLIN

This shy nocturnal mammal covered in scales is a critically endangered species due to urbanisation. When threatened, it will curl up into an armoured ball and fart a horrible smell to keep predators away.

Craft Activity: Plant Press

If you see any interesting leaves or flowers on the ground during your walk, you can keep them in your own DIY Portable Plant Press! Here's what you'll need:

- A long strip of thick cardboard
- 2-3 Rubber bands
- Markers
- Paper (white paper or newspaper)
- Glue stick

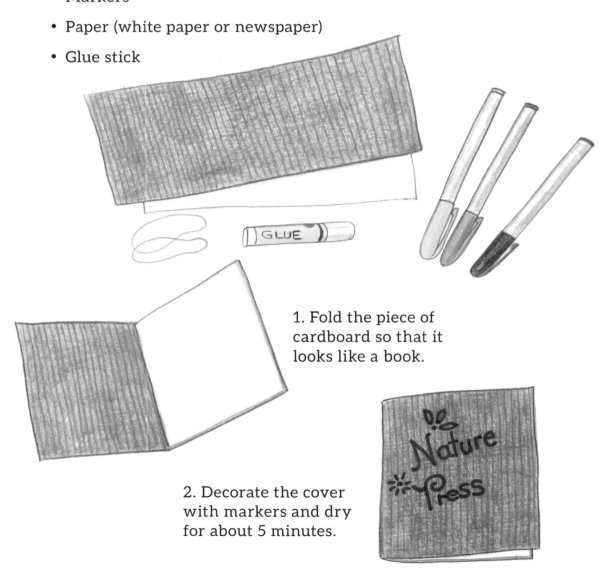

1. Fold the piece of cardboard so that it looks like a book.

2. Decorate the cover with markers and dry for about 5 minutes.

3. Line the inside of the plant press with paper.

4. Rub a glue stick on the corners of the cardboard to keep the paper in place.

5. As you collect plants* during your walk, wrap a couple of rubber bands around your press to keep your pieces of nature flat in place.

6. When you get home, remove the rubber bands and pile a few heavy books on top of your DIY press.

7. In a couple of weeks, they should be dried and pressed. Use them as pretty ornaments for bookmarks or greeting cards.

*Pick only what you find on the ground. It's best to let nature be and not pluck anything from living plants.

Changi Beach Park Intertidal Walk

Along the Changi Beach Park boardwalk is a stretch of lush seagrass meadows (near Changi Carpark 6) which is an intertidal zone – an area that is submerged at high tide but dry and exposed during low tide. It is during the low tide periods where you can find amazing marine life!

THREE TIPS

Go for an intertidal walk during the low tide where more of the shore is exposed – ideally, the tidal height should be 0.2m or below. Check the National Environment Agency (NEA) website (nea.gov.sg/weather/tide-timings) for tide timings.

Don't bring any sea creatures or seashells home, as pretty as they may look. The sea creatures are not likely to survive out of their natural surroundings and shells can be used as homes for the hermit crabs or they break down to form sand on the beach.

Wear covered footwear such as aqua shoes or boots to protect your feet from sharp objects or getting stung by animals.

What can you find here?

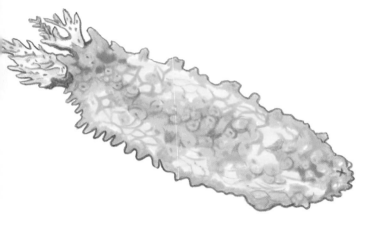

PINK WARTY SEA CUCUMBER

This is probably the first type of creature you will spot during an intertidal walk because of its striking appearance. When threatened by predators, it can vomit out its internal organs and even toxic substances in defence.

BISCUIT SEA STAR

Be careful when handling it! Despite its thick appearance, it is a fragile creature. Don't let it stay out of the water for a long period of time or it will suffocate.

EIGHT-ARMED SEA STAR

This is one of the largest sea star species in Singapore and it is carnivorous, feeding on small creatures such as crustaceans and swallowing them whole.

FLOWER CRAB

It may be hard to spot one as it tends to bury itself in the sand during low tide. However, the male crab has blue markings and attractive patterns on its body. It is also a popular seafood dish in Singapore!

HERMIT CRAB

It cannot grow its own shell. As such, it protects itself by using the empty shells of another animal like a snail. As it grows, it will discard its current shell and search for a larger one.

HADDON'S CARPET ANEMONE

A close relative of coral and jellyfish, this marine animal is covered with short and sticky tentacles. When these tentacles catch a prey, they will guide it to the centre where the anemone's mouth is.

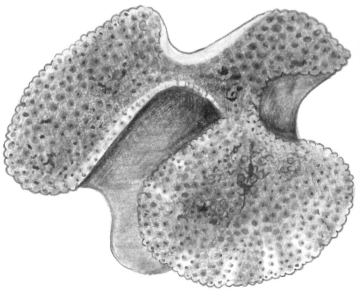

Sungei Buloh Wetland Reserve

AN ECOLOGICAL WONDER

As Singapore's first ASEAN Heritage Park, you will find this sprawling 87-hectare nature park full of rich diversity with mangroves, mudflats, ponds and forests.

There are multiple trails here to explore on boardwalks, along with bird watching pods where you can also cool down in the shade. From September to March, you can catch a diverse range of migrating birds stopping by Sungei Buloh as a pitstop.

Don't forget to get a bird's eye view of the scenic surroundings over at Eagle Point.

What can you find here?

SEA HOLLY

A sprawling shrub that has medicinal properties. For example, juice from the leaves helps to relieve rheumatism.

MANGROVE APPLE

An edible round, green and leathery berry that gives off a sweet pungent smell. Some say it tastes like cheese!

MANGROVE ROOTS

Because a mangrove swamp has a low oxygen level, many plants here have roots that rise above the ground to help them breathe. Look out for knee roots, prop roots, buttress roots and cable roots!

Prop roots

Knee roots

GREY HERON

Sungei Buloh is the only site in Singapore where there's a breeding colony of Grey herons.

GIANT MUDSKIPPER

These are fish that crawl around on mud. They breathe through their wet skin and by retaining water in enlarged gill chambers. Best spotted during low tide!

COLLARED KINGFISHER

They are foodies and eat fish, crustaceans, lizards, snakes, frogs, insects and earthworms.

SALTWATER CROCODILE

If you do spot one, stay calm and keep your distance as it can move really fast and strike when you least expect it.

The Southern Ridges

This 10km hilly trail connects several parks in the Southeast of Singapore and provides plenty of serene views.

Along the way, you'll pass by **Henderson Waves**, the highest pedestrian bridge in this country known for its artistic wave-like structure.

There's also **HortPark**, which resembles a pretty fairytale garden where you can also pick up some tips to care for your plants at home.

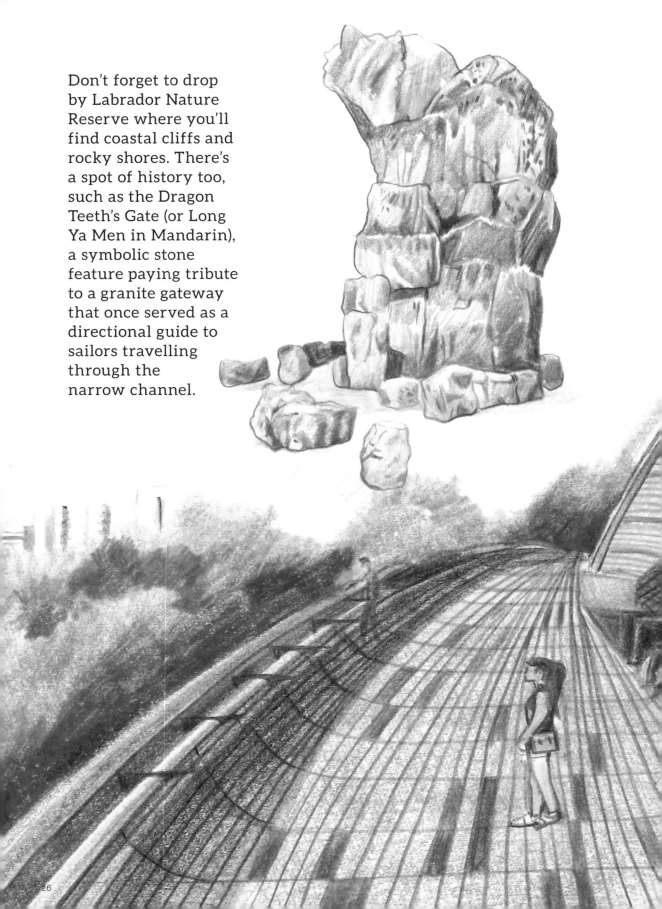

Don't forget to drop by Labrador Nature Reserve where you'll find coastal cliffs and rocky shores. There's a spot of history too, such as the Dragon Teeth's Gate (or Long Ya Men in Mandarin), a symbolic stone feature paying tribute to a granite gateway that once served as a directional guide to sailors travelling through the narrow channel.

Coney Island Park

This offshore 50-hectare island is the perfect cycling spot as the trail is mostly flat and you'll get to enjoy a variety of habitants such as coastal forests, grasslands, mangroves and casuarina woodlands. The easiest way to enter Coney Island is from Punggol Point Park but you can also enter from Lorong Halus Park Connector in Pasir Ris.

Did you know? This is an ecologically sustainable park. The timber from uprooted Casuarina trees here were recycled into park signages, benches and the boardwalk.

Another fun fact: In the early 20th century, this island was owned by Aw Boon Haw and Aw Boon Par – the Tiger Balm brand founders and the ones who also built Haw Par Villa (an attraction we featured in the previous *Out & About in Singapore* book).

Bukit Timah Nature Reserve

Bukit Timah Nature Reserve is Singapore's first forest reserve established in 1883 and like Sungei Buloh, is also an ASEAN Heritage Park. It is here that you will find Singapore's largest surviving primary rainforest with majestic dipterocarp trees towering over you.

It is also here where you can find Singapore's highest hill, **Bukit Timah Hill**, at 163m. The trail to the top can get steep at times, but you should be able to reach the summit in around an hour at a leisurely pace.

For a more relaxing walk, you could head to **Hindhede Nature Park** which is just next to the reserve. There's an easy trail that brings you to Hindhede Quarry where you can look out for birds, fish and squirrels. Many birders like to come here to take photographs of woodpeckers.

Bukit Timah Summit
Ht. 163.63m
Lat. N 1°21'16.85"
Long. E 103° 46'34.95"

PLAYING

Como Adventure Grove

The COMO Adventure Grove Playground at the Singapore Botanic Gardens Gallop Extension is inspired by nature and of course, set in nature as well.

The Banyan Tree Tower has "roots" and "branches" spread across a giant sandpit and if you climb to the top, you can spot birds, squirrels and butterflies.

If swinging is your thing, you can make your way to the Weeping Fig structures with climbing ropes, swings and hammocks.

Don't miss the giant saga seeds and jackfruit structures which you can scramble onto. It's fun to imagine living in a world of giants!

Craft Activity: Popsicle Park

Want to create your own little playground?
Here's what you'll need:

- Coloured popsicle sticks

- Recycled toilet or kitchen rolls

- A large piece of hard cardboard
  as the base

- Craft glue and/or Blu Tack

- Paint and paintbrushes

- Pipe cleaners

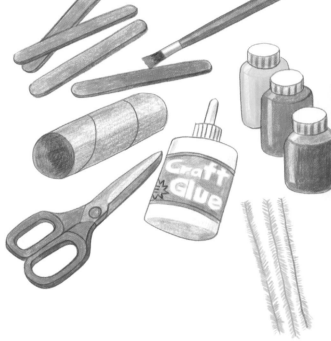

1. Use the popsicle sticks to form the framework of swings, see-saws or any climbing structures you want for your playground. Do get an adult to help if you want to cut the sticks to shorter lengths. You'll need a sharp scissors for that!

2. Cut the cardboard rolls in half to make the swings. Paint them any colour you want!

3. The pipe cleaners can be used as ropes for the swings, or plants around your park.

4. If you have small toy figurines, get them to play in your Popsicle Park as well.

Jurong Lake Gardens

FOREST RAMBLE

The Forest Ramble is a huge playground at Jurong Lake Gardens that is just brimming with fun! There are 13 adventure stations inspired by the animals found in freshwater swamp forests.

You can slither down the snake-like slides...

...or glide across a zipline like a heron and "roost" at the two wooden nests in this play area.

How about pretending to be a frog and bouncing through a series of trampoline pads to get to the other side of the park?

Or you could be a crab, crawling through a maze of wooden tunnels and peering through the clear bubble window as if you're popping out of the sand.

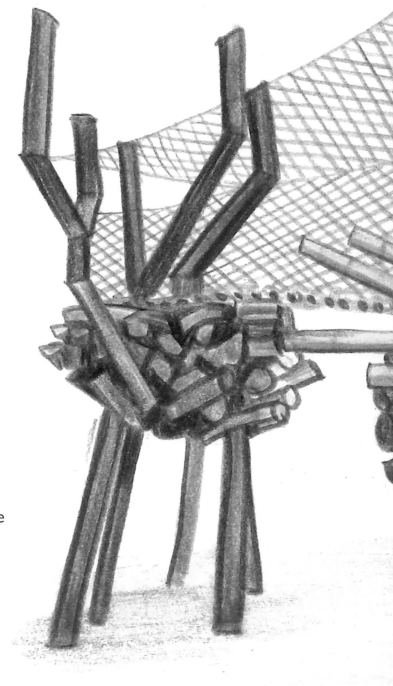

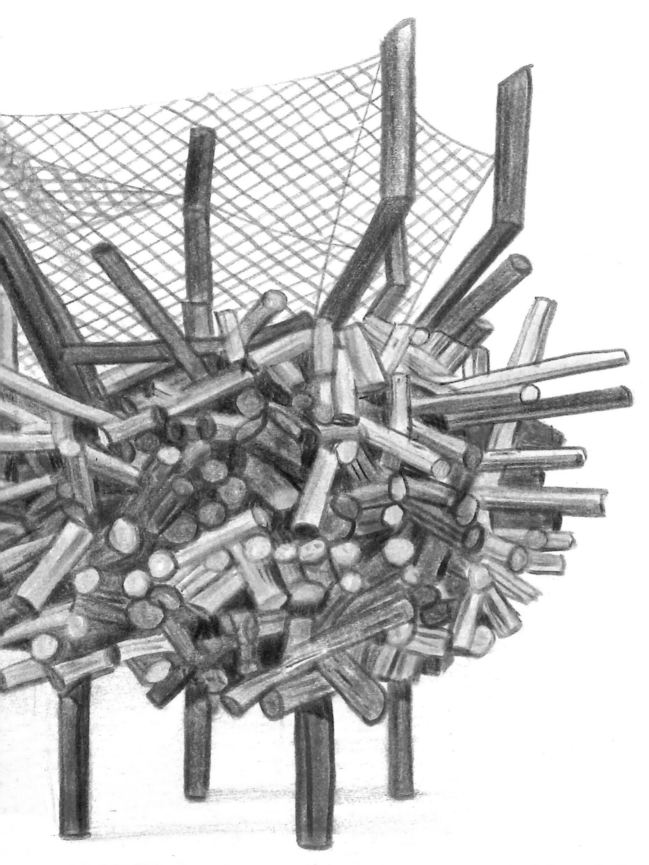

Admiralty Park

SLIDES GALORE!

If you love to play on slides, the Admiralty Park playground is the one for you because it has 26 slides set on a hilly terrain.

The Double Barrel slides are the longest and tallest tube slides found in Singapore's public parks at 23m long and 9m tall.

For a more relaxing ride down, there are also the twin curved roller slides which are the longest outdoor slides in local public parks.

There is even a pair of wide metal slides that allows a family of four to go down together!

Tiong Bahru Park

TILTING TRAIN

The Tiong Bahru Park Playground is built to resemble a tilted train with an engine, three carriages and a caboose (a railway wagon meant for railway workers). You can explore this exciting train through slides, ramps and climbing walls. The challenge is to stay upright as you make your way through the twists and turns of this topsy-turvy structure!

Sembawang Park

BATTLESHIP

Ahoy there! Did you know that in the past, Singapore was a British colony, and British war ships used to dock in Sembawang Naval Base? This impressive playground in Sembawang Park reminds us of this area's history.

PLAYING TO YOUR HEART'S CONTENT

There are many climbing features within this grand wooden structure such as a rock wall, monkey bar, nettings and fireman poles. Look out for the gun-turrets, smokestacks, propellers and a rudder – parts that you would find in a real naval ship.

LEARNING

Science Centre Singapore

The Science Centre Singapore makes science education fun with their creative exhibitions.

For example, the **Earth Alive** interactive exhibits show visitors how the Earth is constantly changing and what causes phenomena such as earthquakes, tsunamis and volcanic eruptions to occur.

Butterflies Up-Close not only shows you how a butterfly grows and behaves, it also has an indoor Live Butterfly Enclosure where you can get up close and personal with these fascinating creatures.

Future Makers introduces visitors to the different fields of engineering, with opportunities to fly a drone or manoeuvre rovers through challenging courses. There's even an Escape Room where you can apply your problem-solving skills to save the world from an alien invasion!

The Science Centre previously exhibited The Human Body Experience, which let visitors imagine they were being swallowed up inside a human body where they could discover how it works.

Edible Garden City

Edible Garden City is a social enterprise that encourages Singaporeans to grow their own food.

During the school break, they usually organise Junior Urban Farmer Holiday Programmes for kids aged from 6-12 where you get to immerse yourself in farm life and be introduced to various plants and animals.

WELCOME TO EDIBLE GARDEN CITY

149 375

www.ediblegardencity.com

In Singapore, most of us live in an urban environment and don't come into much contact with soil or live animals. This programme gives you the opportunity to discover how fulfilling it is to care for flora and fauna.

You'll also be given gardening and composting tips so that you can grow your own edible plants back home! For more information, you can visit their website at http://www.ediblegardencity.com

The team at Edible Garden City also works with companies to design and build rooftop gardens in the city so that office workers can interact with nature.

The Gem Museum

If you have always been fascinated with sparkly things, the Gem Museum is a must-visit! It is a private gems and minerals museum displaying over 700 gem specimens from all over the world.

The museum explains how gems are formed in rocks, where they are mined, and how they are cut and sold. At the end of your visit, you could even buy some gems back home and start a collection.

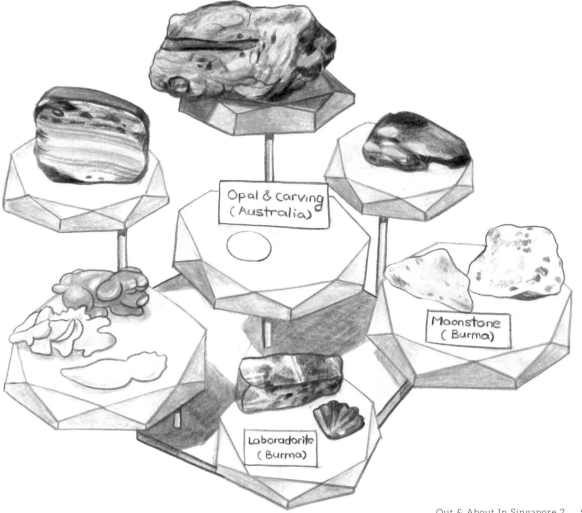

Opal & carving (Australia)

Moonstone (Burma)

Laboradorite (Burma)

Singapore Zoo

The Singapore Zoo is regarded by many as one of the best zoos in the world. Over 4,200 animals reside there.

FEED THE ANIMALS

A fun way to get up close and personal with some of the animals is to book feeding sessions online (http://mandai.com) where you'll learn more about what and how they eat. Feeding the elephants, giraffes and the White rhinoceros can be especially fun!

MEET THE KEEPERS

At certain times of the day, the keepers will come out to tell visitors more about the unique features of the animals that they care for. Meeting keepers is a great opportunity for you to find out more about the animals that you meet – they're usually full of interesting stories!

River Wonders

For more animal fun, there's also River Wonders, which is just a stone's throw away from Singapore Zoo. It is Asia's first and only river-themed wildlife park. Here, you'll come across a wide range of animals you can find in and around rivers across the world.

PANDA PARADISE

At the Yangtse River zone, you may be lucky enough to spot the Giant panda family – Kai Kai, Jia Jia and their baby boy, Le Le – frolicking about with bamboo. (Sometimes, they are shy and like their privacy.) There are also Red pandas in that area!

AMAZING AMAZON

Meanwhile, over at the Amazon Flooded Forest zone, you'll find the world's largest freshwater aquarium where majestic manatees can be found serenely chomping on leaves.

For a bit of thrill, the Amazon River Quest is a 10-minute boat ride that allows you to spot various animals typically found in in the Amazon rainforest such as jaguars and Brazilian tapirs.

Farewell Note

Hi reader,

We hope that going through this book has made you more excited about exploring the natural outdoors in Singapore! And on the rainy or scorching days, we've also suggested a couple of indoor spots where you can learn more about how wondrous Mother Nature is.

You may have heard your teachers and parents talk about how the environment is going through many challenges – climate change, forest wildfires, pollution, endangered animals etc. However, just knowing about these issues is not enough. When we spend time with nature regularly, we begin to experience for ourselves just how beautiful it is, and we'll start to feel more motivated about taking better care of our planet Earth!

PS: We'd love to find out more about what you discover as a Singapore Explorer! You can connect with us on Instagram at @melanderings (Melanie) and @merchantofhappiness (William).

For a start, you can log onto the Clean & Green Singapore website (https://www.cgs.gov.sg) with your parents to find out how you can be more eco-friendly in your everyday life. Just as importantly, keep on staying connected with nature. It's a wonderful way to relax, get healthy, learn new things in fun ways and develop a respectful appreciation of our fellow living beings.

Yours naturally,

Melanie & William

ALSO AVAILABLE